Tell Me Why

WHY?

We Have Tornadoes

Linda Crotta Brennan

Published in the United States of America by Cherry Lake Publishing
Ann Arbor, Michigan
www.cherrylakepublishing.com

Content Adviser: Jack Williams, science writer specializing in weather
Reading Adviser: Marla Conn, ReadAbility, Inc.

Photo Credits: © Pete Pahham/Shutterstock Images, cover, 1, 15; © Dalton Dingelstad/Shutterstock
Images, cover, 1, 21; © Digital Media Pro/Shutterstock Images, cover, 1, 9; © Minerva Studio/Shutterstock
Images, cover, 1, 7; © Alexey Stiop/Shutterstock Images, cover, 1, 17; © John Wollwerth/Shutterstock
Images, cover, 1, 13; © michaeljung/Shutterstock Images, back cover; © Fotokostic/Shutterstock Images,
5; © dalmingo/Shutterstock Images, 9; © Pavel L Photo and Video/Shutterstock Images, 11; © mattgeo/
Shutterstock Images, 15; © Lisa F. Young/Shutterstock Images, 19; © Lisa S./Shutterstock Images, 21

Library of Congress Cataloging-in-Publication Data

Brennan, Linda Crotta, author.
 We have tornadoes / by Linda Crotta Brennan.
    pages cm. -- (Tell me why)
 Summary: "Offers answers to the most compelling questions natural
disasters and weather. Age-appropriate explanations and appealing photos.
Additional text features and search tools, including a glossary and an
index, help students locate information and learn new words"-- Provided by
publisher.
 Audience: Grade K to 3.
 Includes bibliographical references and index.
 ISBN 978-1-63188-012-4 (hardcover) -- ISBN 978-1-63188-055-1 (pbk.) --
ISBN 978-1-63188-098-8 (pdf) -- ISBN 978-1-63188-141-1 (ebook) 1.
Tornadoes--Juvenile literature--Miscellanea. 2. Children's questions and
answers. I. Title.

QC955.2.B74 2015
551.55'3--dc23
                        2014005712

Cherry Lake Publishing would like to acknowledge the work of The Partnership for 21st Century Skills.
Please visit www.p21.org for more information.

Printed in the United States of America
Corporate Graphics Inc.

Table of Contents

No Game Today

"I hear thunder," said Ben.

A big black cloud was heading toward the soccer field.

"That doesn't look good," said his mom.

The referee came up to them. "Sorry. The game is canceled. I just heard an alarm on my weather radio. We have a **tornado watch**. You need to head home right away."

Ben and his mom rushed to the car. He was disappointed he wouldn't be playing a game today. "Why are there tornadoes, anyway?"

Outdoor games are canceled when a tornado is nearby.

A tornado is a fast-spinning tower of air that reaches from a thundercloud to the ground. Tornadoes are more powerful than any other kind of storm. But what causes a tornado?

A tornado reaches from a cloud down to the ground.

Tornado Alley

Tornadoes occur all over the world. But the United States has more tornadoes than any other country. There are about 1,200 in the United States every year.

Most tornadoes happen in an area nicknamed Tornado Alley. This is a flat area between the **Rocky Mountains** and the **Appalachian Mountains**. But tornadoes hit other parts of the country, too.

Rocky Mountains

Appalachian Mountains

LOOK!

What do you see? Do you live near or in Tornado Alley?

The center of the United States has more tornadoes than other areas of the world.

9

As they drove home, Ben frowned. "I wish there weren't any tornadoes during soccer season."

Mom shrugged. "Unfortunately, most of your soccer games are during **tornado season**."

"But wasn't there a tornado near Grandma last November?" asked Ben.

"Most tornadoes hit during tornado season. But they can happen at other times, too," said Mom.

Driving in a storm can be difficult and dangerous.

Warm Air Meets Cold Air

"What causes a tornado?" Ben asked.

"Scientists don't understand exactly how tornadoes form," said Mom. "They usually occur when warm, moist air from the south meets cold, dry air from the north."

The warm and cold winds push each other. This makes the winds turn and spin, sometimes forming a supercell thunderstorm. Supercells are powerful, spinning thunderstorms. They often produce hail, strong winds, and flash floods.

Supercell thunderstorms are more powerful than regular storms.

Supercell storms can create spinning tunnels of air. If one of these tunnels touches the ground, it becomes a tornado.

Suddenly, a news alert came on the radio. "A supercell thunderstorm is headed our way. Take shelter. **Storm spotters** are keeping an eye on the storm."

"What are storm spotters?" asked Ben.

"Storm spotters are trained people who watch storms. They alert authorities if the storms become dangerous." His mom pulled into their driveway. They hurried inside.

What would happen if we didn't have storm spotters to warn us about dangerous storms?

During a tornado watch or warning it is important to take shelter.

Ben turned on the computer. "This Web site says some tornadoes last only a few seconds. Others last more than an hour. Most last about 10 minutes."

"Tornadoes don't last long," said Mom, "but they can do a lot of damage, even in a short period of time."

A tornado destroyed this house and truck.

Staying Safe

"The radio just announced a **tornado warning**," Mom called.

A **meteorologist** had recently visited Ben's school. Ben remembered what to do during a tornado. He put on his bike helmet for head protection. His house didn't have a basement. So he hurried to the first floor bathroom. It didn't have any windows.

Mom brought the weather radio and a couple of sleeping bags. She and Ben pulled the thick sleeping bags over their heads.

The storm roared. Rain beat against the house. Mom held Ben's hand.

Meteorologists use computers to study and track storms.

Then everything got quiet.

"The danger of a tornado has passed," the radio announcer said.

Ben and his mom went outside. There were lots of sticks and even some tree branches in their yard. Ben found a piece of a **shingle** from the roof.

"Luckily, the tornado missed us," said Mom.

Ben grinned. "Maybe tomorrow I'll be able to play soccer."

ASK QUESTIONS

Write a list of three questions about powerful storms. Then go online with an adult or visit your local library to find the answers.

A tornado's wind is strong enough to knock down trees.

Think About It

What if you had a tornado warning in your town? What would you do?

A meteorologist studies much more than tornadoes. Go online with an adult or visit your library to learn more about a meteorologist's job.

Do you think buildings built in Tornado Alley are different from buildings in other areas?

Glossary

Appalachian Mountains (ap-uh-LAY-shun MOUN-tuhnz) a chain of mountains running north to south in the eastern part of the United States

meteorologist (mee-tee-uh-RAH-luh-jist) an expert who studies weather

Rocky Mountains (RAH-kee MOUN-tuhnz) a chain of mountains running north to south in the western part of the United States

shingle (SHING-guhl) a thin, flat piece of wood or other material used to cover roofs

storm spotters (STORM SPAH-terz) trained people who go out and watch storms so they can alert others if the storms become dangerous

tornado season (tor-NAY-doh SEE-zuhn) the time of year when most tornadoes happen, from April to July

tornado warning (tor-NAY-doh WORN-eng) an alert given when a tornado has been spotted and people need to take shelter

tornado watch (tor-NAY-doh WAHCH) an alert given when a tornado is possible, such as when there is a supercell thunderstorm nearby

Find Out More

Books:

Goin, Miriam Busch. *Storms*. Washington, DC: National Geographic Society, 2009.

Martin, Michael. *How to Survive a Tornado*. Mankato, MN: Capstone Press, 2009.

Park, Louise. *Tornadoes*. North Mankato, MN: Smart Apple Media, 2008.

Web Sites:

National Geographic Kids—Forces of Nature: Tornadoes 101
http://video.nationalgeographic.com/video/kids/forces-of-nature-kids/tornadoes-101-kids
Take a tornado quiz and look at photos of tornadoes.

FEMA Ready—Be a Hero
www.ready.gov/kids
Test your knowledge about how to be prepared during a disaster and learn what you should keep in an emergency kit.

Index

About the Author

Linda Crotta Brennan has a master's degree in education. She spent her life around books, teaching, and working at the library. Now she's a full-time writer who loves learning new things. She lives with her husband and golden retriever. She has three grown daughters and a growing gaggle of grandchildren.